W9-BMI-786

# Machines at Work
# School Buses

by Allan Morey

Bullfrog Books

# Ideas for Parents and Teachers

Bullfrog Books let children practice reading informational text at the earliest reading levels. Repetition, familiar words, and photo labels support early readers.

## Before Reading

- Discuss the cover photo. What does it tell them?

- Look at the picture glossary together. Read and discuss the words.

## Read the Book

- "Walk" through the book and look at the photos. Let the child ask questions. Point out the photo labels.

- Read the book to the child, or have him or her read independently.

## After Reading

- Prompt the child to think more. Ask: Have you ever ridden a school bus? Where did you go? What things help keep kids safe on a bus?

Bullfrog Books are published by Jump!
5357 Penn Avenue South
Minneapolis, MN 55419
www.jumplibrary.com

Library of Congress Cataloging-in-Publication Data

Morey, Allan.
  School buses / by Allan Morey.
    pages cm — (Machines at work)
  Includes bibliographical references and index.
  Summary: "This photo-illustrated book for early readers explains the things on a school bus that help keep students safe as they travel to and from school" — Provided by publisher.
  Audience: Grades K-3.
  ISBN 978-1-62031-108-0 (hard cover) —
  ISBN 978-1-62496-174-8 (ebook)
  1. School buses — Juvenile literature.  I. Title.
  TL232.M56 2014
  629.222'33—dc23
                                        2013047727

Series Editor: Wendy Dieker
Series Designer: Ellen Huber
Book Designer: Anna Peterson
Photo Researcher: Kurtis Kinneman

Photo Credits: Andresr/Shutterstock, 20 (boy); Blend Images/SuperStock, 12–13; Brett Critchley|Dreamstime.com, 4; ChrisMilesPhoto/Shutterstock, 10; Don Hammond/Design Pics/Corbis, 12 inset, 23br; Gary Rhijnsburger/Masterfile, 20–21; George Dukinas/Shutterstock, 8 (inset); graytln/iStock, 6, 23tl; Hurst Photo/Shutterstock, 16–17, 18–19; Iris Schneider|Dreamstime.com, 22; Jerry Horbert/Shutterstock, 8–9; Juli Hansen/Shutterstock, 23tl; Le Do/Shutterstock, 24; lev radin/Shutterstock, 23bl; Mari/iStock, 7; MaxyM/Shutterstock, 14–15; monkeybusinessimages, 18 (inset); stevecoleimages/iStock, 21 (inset); rgbspace/iStock, 1; Rob Wilson/Shutterstock, 3; Skypixel|Dreamstime.com, cover; Starletdarlene|Dreamstime.com, 17 (inset), 23tr; Stuart Monk/Shutterstock, 11; Stuart Monk|Dreamstime.com, 5; ZUMA Press, Inc./Alamy, 14 (inset).

Printed in the United States of America at Corporate Graphics, in North Mankato, Minnesota.
3-2014
10 9 8 7 6 5 4 3 2 1

# Table of Contents

# School Buses at Work

Look!

See that yellow bus?
It is a school bus.

Ava waits at a bus stop.

6

The bus will take her safely to school.

# Red lights flash.
# Stop signs pop out.
# They tell cars to stay back.

9

Al drives
the bus.

He opens the door.
The kids get on.

Look! A video camera.

It records kids on the bus.

It makes sure they are safe.

video camera

# The school bus has a back door.

# It is for emergencies.

SCHOOL BUS

EMERGENCY DOOR

BUS EMPTY

TO COMMENT ON MY DRIVING CALL: SCHOOL

204

emergency door

15

Are there other times to ride a school bus?

Yes! On field trips.

Jim's class visits the zoo.

# Now school is over.
# The bus takes kids home.

crossing
bar

The crossing bar sticks out.
Ari walks in front of it.
The driver sees he is safe.
Good night!

# Parts of a School Bus

**flashing lights**
Lights warn other drivers that the bus is stopping.

**stop sign**
The sign tells other drivers to stop so that kids can safely get on or off a school bus.

**crossing bar**
This bar makes sure kids cross in front of the bus where the driver can see them.

SCHOOL BUS

STOP

# Picture Glossary

**bus stop**
A place where kids wait to get on a bus.

**field trip**
A trip students take to a museum, zoo, or other place of learning.

**emergency**
Something dangerous that happens suddenly.

**video camera**
A camera that records moving pictures.

# Index

# To Learn More

Learning more is as easy as 1, 2, 3.

1) Go to www.factsurfer.com

2) Enter "school bus" into the search box.

3) Click the "Surf" button to see a list of websites.

With factsurfer.com, finding more information is just a click away.